THE Internet

Robert Snedden

HODDER
Wayland

An imprint of Hodder Children's Books

Produced for Hodder Wayland by
Discovery Books Ltd
Unit 3, 37 Watling Street, Leintwardine
Shropshire SY7 0LW, England

First published in 2000 by Hodder Wayland,
an imprint of Hodder Children's Books
Paperback edition published in 2001

A catalogue record of this book is available from
the British Library

ISBN 0 7502 2711 7

Printed and bound in Italy by
G.Canale & C.S.p.A, Turin

Designer: Ian Winton
Editor: Gianna Williams
Illustrations: Keith Williams, Ian Heard, Kevin Maddison

Hodder Wayland would like to thank the following for their material: Amazon.co.uk, Ambrosia.com, Ask.com,
CafeInternet, CompuServe, Earthlink, eCash Technologies, Electrolux, Ericsson, eternal.california.com, Geocities.com,
IBM, Musee du Louvre (www.louvre.fr), NASA, Sydney Aquarium, Waterstones, and Yahoo! Davis Station Webcam
appears Courtesy Australian Antarctic Division/Copyright Commonwealth of Australia.

Hodder Children's Books
A division of Hodder Headline Limited
338 Euston Road
London NW1 3BH
England

CONTENTS

INTERNET WORLD

Imagine watching a comet crashing into the atmosphere of Jupiter minutes after it happens rather than having to wait for the next news programme on TV. Imagine seeing what the weather is like in another country, right now. This is already possible with the Internet.

Virtual visitors

Every year five million tourists visit the Louvre Museum in Paris. Double that number visit the Louvre website on the Internet.

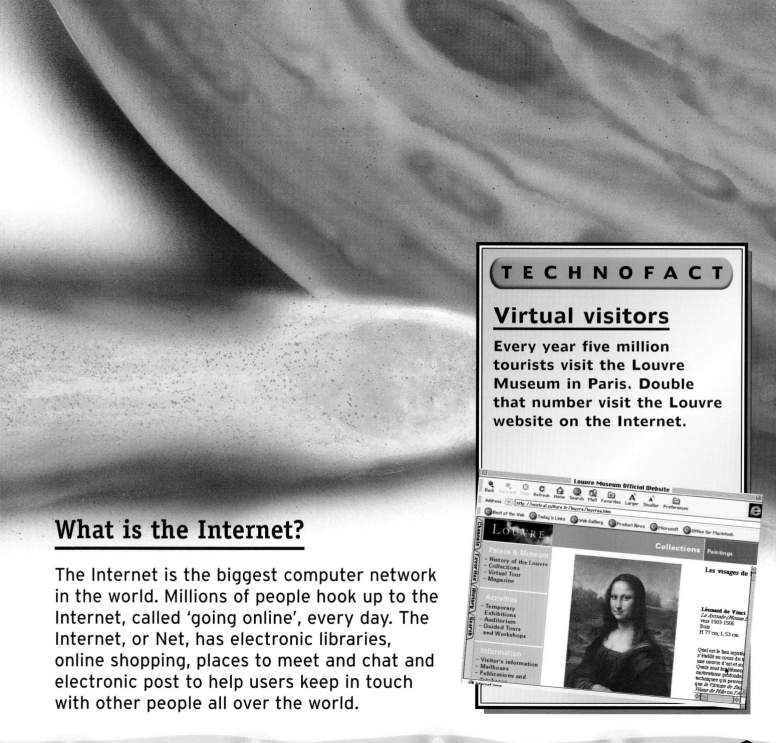

What is the Internet?

The Internet is the biggest computer network in the world. Millions of people hook up to the Internet, called 'going online', every day. The Internet, or Net, has electronic libraries, online shopping, places to meet and chat and electronic post to help users keep in touch with other people all over the world.

THE INTERNET STORY

In the 1960s the US Defense Department invented a system to link together their computers. They wanted to create a communications system that would stay running even if one or more of its links were destroyed.

Explosive growth

At first this computer network, the ARPANET (Advanced Research Projects Agency Network), had just four computers linked together. By the beginning of 1996 around 9.5 million computers were connected to the Internet. Today no one knows how many millions of people access the Internet every day.

Who runs the Internet?

No one person or organization decides what will be on the Internet. Cyberspace, or the online world, is created day by day by the people who use it.

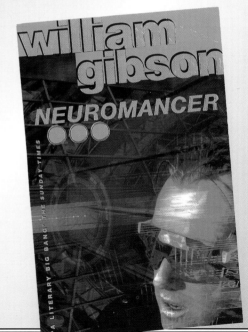

GOING ONLINE

The Internet is available to everyone with a computer and a phone line. It makes use of the same worldwide network of phone lines and satellite links that carry telephone calls.

▶ Your computer is your gateway to the online world.

Modems

A device called a modem, which can either be inside or outside your computer, plugs into the telephone socket, just like an ordinary phone does. The modem changes computer information into a form that can be carried over a telephone line. It also changes it back again.

Graphics, sound and animation are all part of the online experience.

Online services and service providers

To get online, your computer needs to call another computer already linked to the Internet. This could be an online service, such as AOL (America On Line), or an Internet service provider (ISP). An online service gives access to its own network of facilities.

An online service provides more than just a link to the Internet. News, shopping, games and more are all on offer as well as an Internet connection.

ELECTRONIC MAIL

The most popular reason for being online is electronic mail, or e-mail. This is a message you send from your computer to any other computer anywhere in the world. E-mail is inexpensive and it can be with the other person in seconds.

An e-mail is sent from a computer via a modem down a telephone line, and then sent via satellite across the world. A phone line is linked to a satellite ground station.

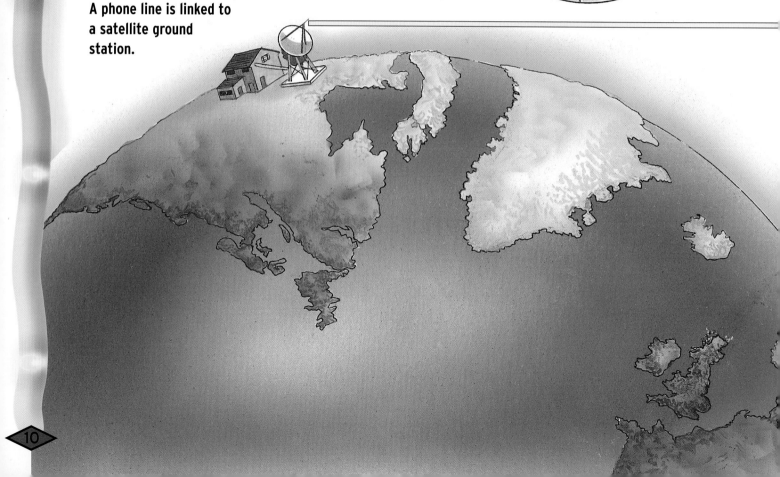

How e-mail works

To send and receive e-mail you must have a connection to the Internet and access to a computer called a mail server. Having a mail server address is like having a house address where people can send you regular mail.

A satellite relays the message to another ground station.

T E C H N O F A C T

E-mail addresses

Everyone with access to the Internet has an e-mail address. E-mail addresses have two parts separated by an @ sign. To the left of the sign is the user's name, to the right is the name of the computer that holds their e-mail account.

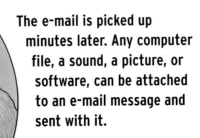

The e-mail is picked up minutes later. Any computer file, a sound, a picture, or software, can be attached to an e-mail message and sent with it.

NEWSGROUPS

Ever wanted to ask a question but didn't know who to ask? What if you like to go mountain biking and you want to ask someone what the best tyres are for muddy terrain? If you are on the Internet you can ask your question on a newsgroup.

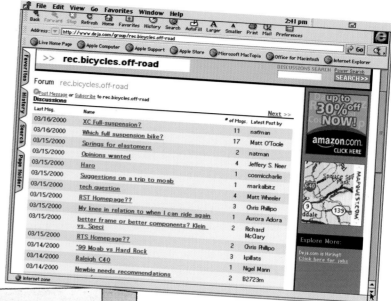

Newsgroups are places where people can discuss a huge variety of different topics.

Pick a topic

Newsgroups are set up by groups of people who post messages to each other about topics that interest them. The newsgroup network, called Usenet, is made up of a huge number of electronic discussion groups.

Spreading the word

When you post an article to a newsgroup, it goes first to your local news server, which might be at your service provider or at your school. Your server then sends copies of the article to other servers. Soon there are thousands of copies of the article on servers all over the world.

THE WORLD WIDE WEB

An amazing amount of information and entertainment in words, pictures and sounds is stored on the World Wide Web. The Web is a collection of millions of different documents called Web pages which can be seen on the Internet. Web pages are stored on many different computers all over the world.

Surfing the Net

To get on to the Web you need a Web browser, such as Netscape Navigator or Microsoft Internet Explorer. A browser is a piece of software that can display Web pages on your screen. Web pages are written in a computer language called Hypertext Mark-up Language, or HTML. Web files are linked together by hypertext, which allows you to jump from place to place on the Web. This is called browsing or surfing the Net.

1. On the first page of the Sydney Aquarium website, the left-hand column has a list of contents. Click on Quick Tour with your mouse.

Welcome to Sydney Aquarium

Back Forward Stop Refresh Home Search Mail Favorites Larger Smaller Preferences

Address: http://www.sydneyaquarium.com.au/home.html

Best of the Web   Today's Links   Web Gallery   Product News   Microsoft   Office for Macintosh

Channels   Favorites   History   Search

Sydney Aquarium

Tentacle Links

Educational Resources

Fin News

Info Center

Ocean Gallery

Quick Tour

QUICK TOUR

FIN NEWS

INFO CENTRE

Welcome to the Sydney Aquarium, recognised internationally as one of the world's Great Aquariums.

[Quick Tour] [Fin News] [Info Centre] [Educational Resources]

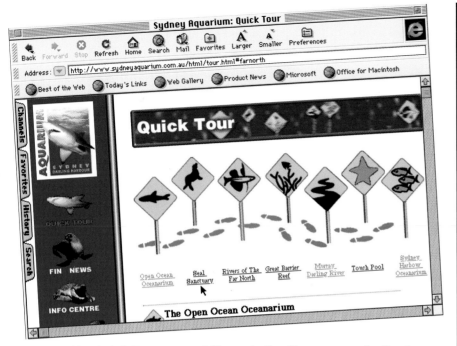

2. On the Quick Tour page of the website, there are underlined words called hypertext links. If you click on one with a mouse, it will take you to another page of the website.

3. It is hard to get lost in a website. There is usually a 'home' link to get back to the beginning of the site and a list of other pages.

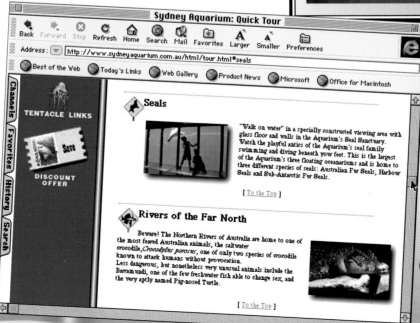

SEARCHING

There are millions of pages of information on the Web. You could easily spend days trying to find something. Searching the Internet requires patience, luck, skill and a lot of help from a search engine!

How?

A search needn't be limited to one search engine. Websites such as AskJeeves and Mamma, or Apple's Sherlock program, will try several search engines at once for you.

Search engines

There are dozens of these to help you find what you're looking for, such as HotBot, Yahoo!, AltaVista, Infoseek and others. Search engines come in two basic types – directories and indexes. Directories group websites under headings, such as museums or baseball teams. When you use a Web index it will find individual pages of a website that match your search.

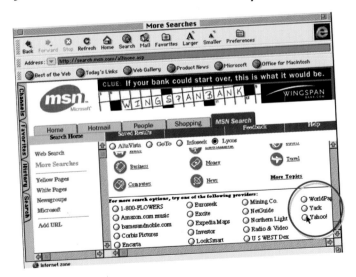

1. On the home page of your service provider are the names of several different search engines. Select the one you want by clicking on it.

Spiders on the Web

A Web index, such as AltaVista, uses software programs called spiders or robots that go through millions of Web pages and newsgroup postings, indexing all of the words that match a search.

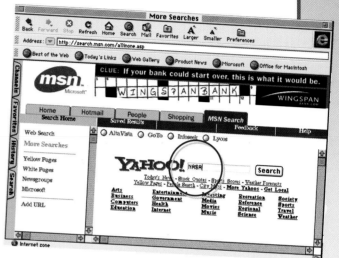

2. On the search engine page, type the name of what you are looking for in the empty box and ask for a search.

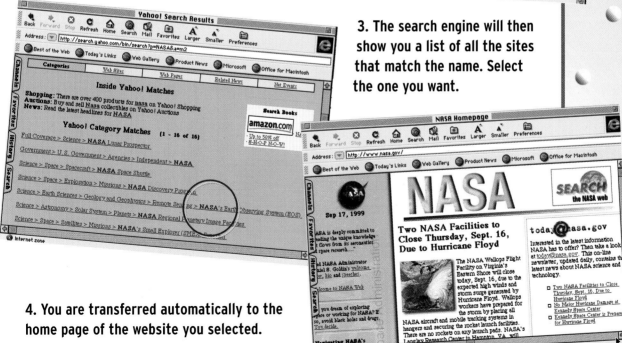

3. The search engine will then show you a list of all the sites that match the name. Select the one you want.

4. You are transferred automatically to the home page of the website you selected.

MULTIMEDIA ONLINE

Wouldn't it be wonderful to call a friend on the other side of the world and be able to see them talking to you at the same time? This is already possible thanks to the Internet.

Using the Internet it is possible to see and hear people on your computer in real time.

Can you see me?

CU-SeeMe, developed at Cornell University in the United States, is a free video-conferencing program that lets people send and receive video and sound over the Internet. Groups of people can talk to one another using microphones and speakers attached to their computers, while pictures of group members appear on the screen.

Turn on and tune in

Multimedia programs combine sound, still and moving pictures and text. You can download multimedia files from the Net. Anyone with a fast modem and a powerful enough computer can play live audio and video. You can tune into radio stations and video cameras linked up to the Net from all over the world.

Davis Station, Antarctica

Address: http://www.antdiv.gov.au/stations/davis/video.html

Best of the Web   Today's Links   Web Gallery   Product News   Microsoft   Office for Macintosh

Davis Station Webcam, Antarctica

Davis 17 September   4:00 PM

What's Happening

Mid winters darts match at Davis Station. Click here for more information

Weather

Outside air temperature is -8.3 degrees C, wind speed is 7 knots or 12 km/hr.

Internet zone

A video camera connected to the Internet is called a webcam. A webcam lets people see live pictures when they visit the website.

WORK AND PLAY

Now you can buy more and more products without ever leaving the chair in front of your computer screen. Many thousands of companies already sell their goods and services on the Web.

▶ It's simple to buy plane tickets on the Internet.

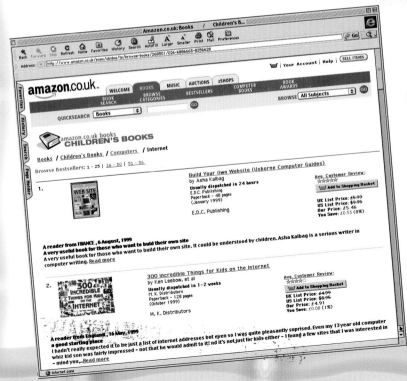

Some shops allow customers to select products on the Net and then deliver them to their home. Goods are paid for by credit card.

Amazon is an online bookshop. Books can be bought with a credit card and are delivered soon after.

T E C H N O F A C T

Global market

Web experts have predicted that there may be as many as 500 million people on the Net by 2001. That's a lot of people to sell to!

Electronic money

Some companies have developed electronic money or eCash. With eCash, you withdraw digital money from an Internet bank account just as you would real money from a real bank. Instead of having it in a purse or wallet it is stored on your computer. When you want to pay for something, you send the cybershop eCash straight from your computer.

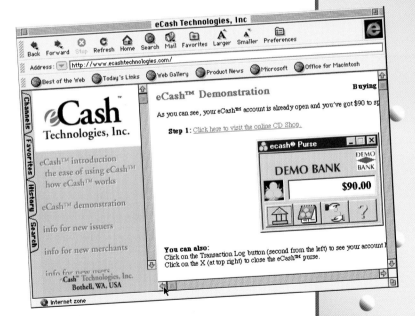

eCash systems might make buying and selling over the Internet easier and safer.

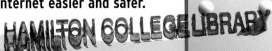

FUN AND GAMES

There are many fun things to do on the Net. There are a huge number of games that you can download to your computer, for example. Better yet, there are games that can be played with other people online.

Downloading

There are many kinds of games on the Net which you can find with the help of a search engine. Once you find a game you like, you can download it to your computer. That means that you can then play the game whenever you like without having to get back online.

Online gaming

A number of sites on the Internet let you play games with other players around the world. These range from traditional games like chess and backgammon to role-playing games where players can play in teams in a fantasy world.

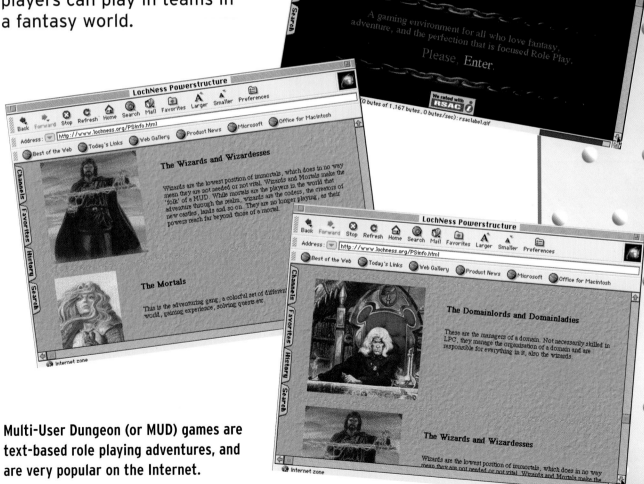

Multi-User Dungeon (or MUD) games are text-based role playing adventures, and are very popular on the Internet.

CHAT

When you visit a chat room, you can talk to other people while they are online, no matter where they are in the world. If you have a friend that lives in another country, you can arrange to meet at a certain chat room and talk to each other there.

You don't need to own a computer to surf the Net. Internet cafés let you go online and have a snack at the same time.

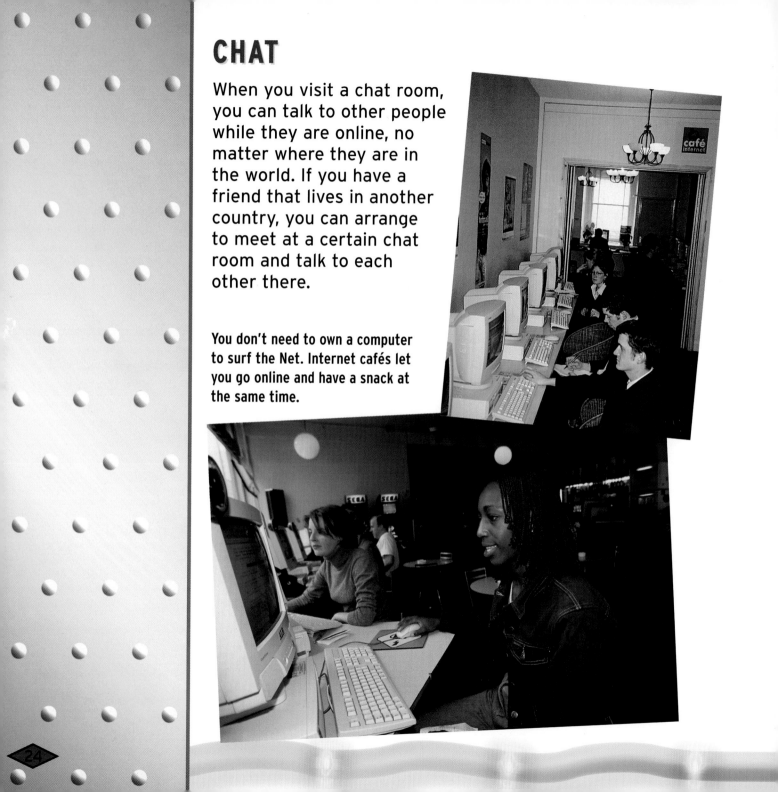

Chat rooms

Chat rooms work like telephone conversations but with lines of text instead of voices. Many websites now have chat rooms. Online services such as AOL provide areas for members to chat with each other on different topics. Other Internet users can chat using servers such as Internet Relay Chat (IRC).

◀ This bookshop offers Internet browsing to all its customers.

NET SPEAK

Net users are constantly inventing new expressions to speed up their chat. An online conversation could well go something like this:

J: Hi there, my name is Joe. I'm a **newbie** and I need some help with the Internet.

newbie - *new user*

S: Hi Joe, I'm Sara. How did you find out about this chat room?

J: **FOAF**. Well actually it was my dad.

FOAF - *friend of a friend*

S: **LOL**. Your dad?!

LOL - *laugh out loud*

J: Actually, he's cool. He's a great plumber. Would you like a quote for a new bathroom – he's very reasonable.

S: Is this **spam**?! Get out of our chat room!

Spam - *posting unwanted advertisements*

Lurkers

You don't have to join in with chat and newsgroup discussions. Many people just read what others are saying without responding to it. This is called lurking!

D: Hey, Sara, what's all this **flame** for?

Flame - *angry messages*

S: Dave, look out for a guy called Joe.

D: Hey, Joe, we don't want a **flame war** here. Move on!

Flame war - *a long and angry argument*

J: Sorry Sara, actually I was just throwing in some **flame bait** – this chat room was looking a little boring while I was lurking yesterday.

Flame bait - *outrageous comment designed to get attention*

S: You troll!

Troll - *someone who deliberately starts a flame war*

J: Well, I gotta go. **BCNU**

BCNU - *be seein' you (goodbye)*

Caution!

Just because something appears online it does not mean that what it says is accurate. Anyone with a computer and a modem can write on the Internet, on chat lines, newsgroups and Web pages. Always be wary of what you read on the Net.

WIRED WORLD

Working away from an office, or teleworking, is becoming more common. People can now get on the Internet wherever they are. You can already link mobile phones to laptop computers. Some companies are producing screen phones, helping people get on the Net without a computer.

The Internet allows home computers to be linked to computers at work, making working away from the office easy.

Cool connections

The 'smart house', where you can control household appliances such as your washing machine via the Internet may not be too far off.

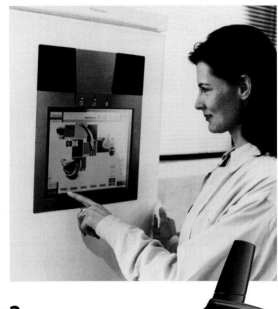

This ScreenFridge can display a shopping list of what is running short. The list can then be sent over the Internet to a supermarket.

The future?

In the future the Internet will be able to carry even greater amounts of data. When that happens, interactive television, movies-on-demand and 3D video-conferencing will be readily available.

WAP mobile phones allow you to get on to the Internet when you are on the move.

GLOSSARY

cyberspace The online world of the Internet.

download To copy information from a computer on the Internet to your own computer.

e-mail (electronic mail) Messages sent to other people via the Internet.

HTML (Hypertext Mark-up Language) The computer language that is used to write pages for the World Wide Web.

hypertext The links between one World Wide Web page and another.

IRC (Internet Relay Chat) A way of chatting to other people on the Internet.

ISP (Internet Service Provider) A company that provides access to the Internet.

mail server A central computer that handles the sending or receiving of e-mail.

modem A device that allows information to be sent back and forth between computers along telephone lines.

multimedia A combination of text, sound and video.

newsgroups A discussion group on Usenet; places where people can exchange ideas on a wide variety of different topics.

online Connected to a computer network.

online service A commercial service that provides many of its own special areas, such as chat and shopping, as well as a link to the Internet.

satellite An object, often man-made, in orbit around a planet.

search engine A program that allows you to search for particular topics on the Internet.

software A program which tells a computer what to do.

teleworking Working away from the office while keeping in touch electronically via computer, fax and so on.

WAP (Wireless Application Protocol) A mobile phone that allows users to link to the Internet.

web browser An application that allows your computer to read the documents on the World Wide Web.

webcam (web camera) A camera that sends pictures to the Internet via a computer.

World Wide Web (WWW) The multimedia part of the Internet, a network of millions of documents joined together by hypertext links.

FURTHER READING

Oxlade, Chris, *20th Century Inventions: Telecommunications*, Wayland, 1996
Wingate, Philippa, *The Internet for beginners: Usborne Computer Guides*,
   Usborne Publishing Ltd, 1997

WEBSITES

www.digitalcentury.com/encyclo/update/comp_hd.html
www.ipl.org/youth/
www.robertniles.com/data
www.ala.org/parentspage/greatsites/science.html

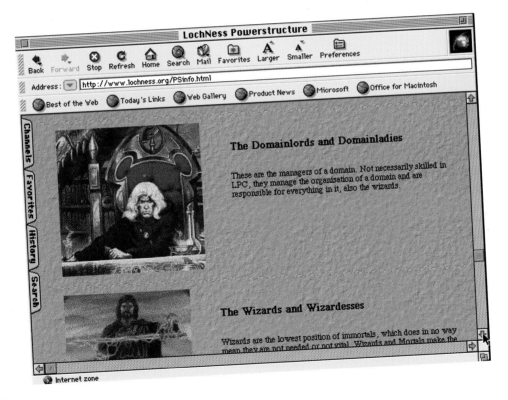

Picture acknowledgements:
8 top M Tcherevkoff/Image Bank, 8 bottom Jerrican Gable/Science Photo Library, 15 Hank Morgan/Science Photo Library, 18 Steve Niedorf/Image Bank, 24 Inge Yspeert/Corbis

INDEX